THE ONLY WAY TO LIVE

A Practical Christian Guide to Constant Inner Peace

DAVE BOURLAND

CHART HOUSE PRESS

The Only Way to Live

First Edition by Dave Bourland

© 2014

ISBN: 978-1-63125-009-5

Chart House Press, LLC.
P O Box 17059
Sugar Land, TX 77469-7059
281-752-6565

www.ChartHousePress.com

Graphic Design: Christy Fuselli
Edited by: Shelly Davis
Additional Writing and Editing: Tiffany Plunkett
Book Design: Megan LaFollett

DEDICATION

I dedicate this book to my wife Rosie, who has been with me through many ups and downs, and has never wavered…

I love you!

A MESSAGE FROM THE PUBLISHER

I believe there are some people who come into our lives for a reason. They may only be with us for a moment, while others are meant to be in our lives forever. We may not understand why our paths crossed at that moment and it could take years before we understand the true meaning or significance of the event. All we know is because of our relationship, conversation or even few seconds in passing, the course of our life has been changed forever.

When David and Rosie Bourland came into my life in 1996, I knew my career would change and I would have the opportunity to develop professionally as never before. But looking back now, I realize the changes in my professional life were only the tip of the iceberg. If you have ever had the pleasure of meeting the Bourlands, you will know from the introduction that they are special.

Rosie is seriously one of the nicest, most loving people you will ever meet. She is just as beautiful on the inside as she is on the out. Like me, David is a dreamer and loves to live life to the fullest. Rosie keeps David grounded while he likes to try new things which, from time to time, may take Rosie out of her comfort zone. They respect each other's differences and take an interest in each other which keeps them balanced and their marriage strong. However, even with their differences, there are two things they both love more than anything else in the world: boating and our Lord Jesus Christ.

I've always considered myself a good Christian. Unfortunately, for most of my life, I don't think I was much different than most Christians. Going to church occasionally, viewing Christianity like a "check the box" list of things to do or not to do. And then God shows up and tries to get your attention. For some people, all He has to do is send one of His living disciples your way to deliver a message. But not for me; I'm stubborn. I'm the type of person that challenges God. The type of person that after sending countless messages with no response, He has to whop on the head a few times and bring me to my knees before I see the Glory. And He did that in 2004 when I worked for Dave.

David brought me into his office for a talk. He said, "Jeff, I truly appreciate you and how hard you are working in my office. You remind me of myself when I was your age and it actually scares me." Well, that was a great compliment, but why in the heck would it scare him? I thought, what in the world is this leading up to? Is he going to fire me for working too hard? I'm tired and just want to get back to my office and finish this PowerPoint for our class tonight! He continued, "You know I used to work like that. All hours of the night, just trying to prove to the world I had what it took to be successful. But then I realized that success wasn't what I thought it would be. Sure, I like nice things and Ro and I love spending time on the boat. But there was a time when I realized I was *too* focused on making money and building a business. There has to be balance in your life and God has to be at the center at all times."

I just stared at the floor, realizing he was right. I knew in my heart that I was placing my work in front of everything else. Though I didn't know it at the time, the change in my life began then: A change to Faith as my priority, followed by family, friends and my career.

Over the years I witnessed David Bourland's impact on people's lives. I could tell you countless stories of what he has done for me and others, but there is one that stands out from the rest. And until now, he has never known that I witnessed his generosity. I came to work one day and as usual, said "Hi" to the security guard who protected the building. I had never taken the time to get to know him, and as he approached me, I could tell something had happened.

With a tear in his eye, he said "I just want to tell you something about your boss and what he just did for me. I received a phone call that I was being evicted from my apartment because I was a few months behind on my rent. He noticed I was upset and asked what had happened. I was embarrassed but told him the story. Can you believe he not only gave me enough money for rent, he's also bought me a car that runs?" The guard began crying uncontrollably. "And when I told him how much I appreciate what he had done, he just hugged me and said, 'Give the glory to God'. Please don't tell him I told you. He asked that I keep it to myself. I just wanted to tell you how amazing he is."

David Bourland is not just a Christian who does good deeds. He is a disciple of Christ who leads by example each and every day. I know he's not perfect and he will be the first person to tell you about mistakes he's made in his life, but he is as good as they come.

When you read his powerful message about the importance of keeping God central in his life, listen and take notes. Seek one of His disciples on earth and allow them to mentor you as I have allowed David to mentor me. My hope and prayer for you is that you hear David's message. Not just the words, but the meaning behind them, and allow him to make a difference in your life as he has in mine.

David and Rosie, thank you for being there for me throughout all these years. Even when you knew I had made poor decisions, you loved me unconditionally and accepted me with open arms. I love both of you dearly and am so proud to have the opportunity to help you deliver your message to the world.

May God continue to bless you,

Jeff Hastings
President, Chart House Press

CONTENTS

FOREWORD

Intelligence, patriotism, Christianity and firm reliance on Him, who has never yet forsaken this favored land, are still competent to adjust in the best way, all our present difficulty.

- Abraham Lincoln -

H istory shows that discipline and high moral principles (or values) can produce great societies; by contrast, a lack of discipline and lax morality can destroy societies. Our founding fathers spoke often of those principles and standards that became the foundation for this great nation. They also spoke often of their faith in God and the Bible. George Washington even wrote, "It is the duty of nations to acknowledge the providence of Almighty God, to obey His will, to be grateful for His benefits and humbly to implore His protection and favor."

Those who founded the United States made it

clear that only with God's help could human beings build a great nation. This is the underlying belief system that sustains our country, because it's the way we started as a nation. Our forefathers' kind of inner discipline and their high moral standards have set the level to which we must return if we are to survive the present and flourish in the years to come.

In the Bible, we see the wisdom that guided our forefathers. The Bible is the foundation we need to live life. It's explicit with regard to how we should live, and if we live according to these principles, we are not confused or lost—even when our flawed world gives us problems and heartaches. Our morals are clear, our discipline strong.

The most exciting, rewarding, fulfilling, fun and joyous life is living daily under God's continual blessing and guidance. It really is the only way to live!

I have lived, Sir, a long time, and the longer I live, the more convincing proofs I see of this truth--that God governs in the affairs of men. And if a sparrow cannot fall to the ground without His notice, is it probable that an empire can rise without His aid?

-Ben Franklin-

INTRODUCTION

You make known to me the path of life; you will fill me with joy in your presence, with eternal pleasures at your right hand.

-Psalm 16:11-

E ach day is a journey to discover who you are and what you can achieve. When you're a child first wondering at the world, the future path of your life seems to go on forever. As you get older, the past is marked with the signs of the Values, Ideas and Things with which you've experimented. It's easy to get lost on that road—but when I was six years old, my mother gave me a map that has guided me ever since.

The map is the Bible.

I believe people tend to minimize how practical the Bible is. It's an amazing, magical book, and much of how it can guide us was lived out for me by my mother.

In my mother's life, I've seen how the Bible provides a firm foundation for our values, leads us to ideas that help us improve ourselves and can help us determine the things that will bring us a lifetime of inner peace — not just a temporary happiness.

The Bible my mother shared with me makes it clear that the more we are in God's presence, the more peace we can have.

I've seen the truth of it in other people over the years — people who, like my mother, learned to keep the presence of God inside their hearts so that they can access it throughout the day.

I'm not saying that God's presence makes them happy all the time. Life doesn't work that way. We all have highs and lows — but even at their lowest moments, those who live with God live in a state of joy.

On that special day in Dallas, Texas, when my mother brought me to God, she gave me the greatest gift of my life. She gave me the answer to living a life of joyous peace.

My mother isn't perfect. Neither am I. We've both made lots of mistakes, but for both of us, the constant presence of God has guided us over those bumps in the road. In fact, without Christ daily helping me moment by moment, I believe I would be in too much fear and worry to be able to successfully deal with the day-to-day pressures of living. But with Christ and

God's peace, I persevere, I grow, and I try to help others.

If you're reading this book, perhaps you're seeking the same kind of peace I found through my mother's life, the Bible and God's presence. So let's take a look at the only way to live.

You keep him in perfect peace whose mind is stayed on you, because he trusts in you.
- Isaiah 26:3-

Chapter I

The Foundation of My Faith

The mind governed by the flesh is death, but the mind
governed by the Spirit is life and peace.

- Romans 8:6 -

The Father Who Wasn't

I stood there in disbelief as I watched my father drag my mother across the floor by her hair. He was strong. He yelled at her, slapped her repeatedly. I was ten. I couldn't understand what was happening. Up to that point I had been aware of sounds and yells behind closed doors, but this was different and it was happening before my eyes. Even at only ten, I was the oldest child. I desperately felt it was my job to *do* something, but all I could do was cry and scream for him to stop. When he wouldn't listen, we cried out to God for help.

And God helped us. My dad left the house. My mother and I prayed together with all our hearts. Mom and I had spent a lot of time in church together and we knew how to call out to God. We reached out to Him, and God removed our fears and gave us peace.

In the calm of Christ's peace, I was able to ask myself an important question: How could anyone cause others physical pain, especially to someone they said they loved? As I prayed by my mother's side for guidance, I realized that I'd just established one of my own values. I would not treat people the way my father abused my mother... ever.

Over the years since then (and there have been many of them!), I've met hundreds of people with similar stories. Whether it was their pain or the pain of someone close to them, they've found that living daily with the spirit of Christ in their hearts gives them the calmness they need to find their way. It's too easy to lose your temper or be overcome with despair sometimes—all of us have had those moments, right? But when you feel as if you're losing yourself to your emotions, step back into the embrace of God's presence. Say His Name, find a piece of quiet in your soul, and you can weather any storm. This was the lesson I learned that day on my knees, praying with my mother.

Like most kids, I'd never asked my mom about what her life was like when she was younger. You don't think of your parents that way. It was later that I found out she was so beautiful in those days that even the most handsome men couldn't resist her laugh or her smile as she played tennis in the hot Texas summers.

I also didn't know that my mother had a secret. It was a few days after my father had left my mother crying in the kitchen when she called me out to the back porch. We sat on the steps, and she told me that my father — was not my father.

The story came out slowly, but she never hesitated. The man I'd known as my father was really my stepfather, who'd adopted me when I was four years old, too young to remember. My real father had been on the east coast for five years, but now he was back in town.

All of a sudden, I wasn't Charles David Jacobs. She told me my real name was Glenn David Bourland, Jr. I didn't know what to expect from my real father. I didn't know what to say to my mother. She and I hugged and cried together, then when I went to my room, I cried the rest of the day. I wouldn't take back my birth name as my own until years later, in 1971.

I know how devastating broken families are for children. I believe many never fully recover from the trauma, as if something stays broken inside. But somehow in the shock of that day, there were still pieces of the puzzle of my life that came together and resolved troubling questions I was too young to voice. Now I realized why I looked so different from my "dad" and why I had different hobbies and interests than he did. He was very strong, an Oklahoma boy with a sixth-grade education who could easily beat other men in a fight. His life had not been gentle, and neither was he—when he started his own concrete company, he was a hard worker but a hard boss too. And apparently he wasn't my father.

Though it had come through a dramatic and unexpected revelation, God was working to help me understand who I really was and to give my mother peace in at last being able to unburden herself. The truth hurt, but it set us free.

Have you had that moment? Something you discovered that wounded you, shocked you, made you feel as if you'd been seeing the world wrong? Most of us have. I wish the only time that had happened to me were that once on the porch when I was ten. But the world isn't perfect and neither are we. That's for Heaven and God. There are constant problems in life and sometimes they are piled up so high that we are overwhelmed. But in those hard years, my mother showed me that by living one moment at a time in close communication with God, we can strive for perfection and He will give us strength to dust ourselves off and try again if we fail.

When You Turn on a Light, the Darkness Goes Away

At some point in our lives, each of us feels empty inside. Maybe we're at a life crossroads, or maybe like my mother and stepfather, we've made bad decisions in the past that come back to haunt us. Recognizing that as a moment of potential growth is hard. So instead, we try to fill the emptiness we sometimes feel inside with things of the flesh, or carnal world, not the spiritual. My stepfather—who I'd thought my whole life was my father—filled his emptiness with anger and worry. It took my mother and the Bible for him to learn that to be in God's presence is the clear way to have spiritual peace, to be free of fear and worry.

Choosing to make God a part of you isn't a *leap* of faith. There's no danger, no sudden moment. Living with God in you is a *walk* of faith, and it works. People who live this way have a much better chance to be in balance, to have stability in their lives, because they are never truly alone. I have been by the side of the sick and the dying, of the lost and those left behind, and I have seen how God's power works inside us to strengthen us so that we can survive the hard times *while* we live a peaceful, fulfilled life. You don't have to wait until the physical world gets better; you can have joy in your heart always. This is the power that frees addicts from addictions, that moves people from bondage to freedom and helps them have an abundant, exciting life of purpose and hope.

My mother knew this. I learned from her in those years, as she protected her family and cemented her faith and brought my stepfather to church. We were raised in an Assembly of God Church (Pentecostal) back in the days of long revivals that lasted for weeks, jumping up and down services and "Jericho Marches" with instruments around the inside and outside of the church. We sat on long wooden pews, and when my stepfather came to God and accepted Him in his heart, he would share a hymnal with us and belt out "Onward Christian Soldiers" as loud as anyone. Our life at home improved even as the house filled with more children. Those were mostly happy years. He worked in the church and taught Sunday School.

But as I said, we live in an imperfect world of imperfect people. Not only did my stepfather leave the church, but he left my mother for another woman, walking away from all responsibilities and seven children.

The Strength That Made Her Stronger

His faith may have weakened, but my mother's

never did. She raised all seven of us with little to no financial help from him, working hard, sometimes with two jobs and keeping things together with God's help. She had amazing energy and made sure we were in church at least twice a week. Because she relied heavily on her faith in God, the Lord blessed her with the strength and peace she needed to get through each day. He didn't always solve her problems, but because of the strength and inner peace her faith gave her, she was able to ensure that we always had food and clothing and love. Most importantly, she gave us a spiritual foundation for our values that money can never buy.

We all have people whose lives of strength and resilience we admire (and sometimes envy, if we're honest). But they've learned those strengths through hardship or challenge just as all of us do. There have been many people who were great examples of God's power in a life to make it through the tough times. My mom has been a great example of surviving through hard difficulties.

For me, my mother is the example of how things work when God is constantly in your heart and mind, but the directions for how to do that are in that amazing map, the Bible. Look again at Isaiah 26:3 and Romans 8:6. Let this become the foundation of your faith as it has become mine. We can learn to keep our mind on Christ. We can stay in His presence and we can have fullness of joy within. But how can we keep our mind on Him and develop the spiritual mind when we have so many other things troubling our minds each day?

CHAPTER II

GOD'S PROMISE TO YOU

And now that you belong to Christ, you are the true
children of Abraham. You are his heirs, and God's
promise to Abraham belongs to you.

- Galatians 3:29 -

L et me give you an example of what happens when you expect too much from things you can't control. In first grade I was a class cut-up, definitely outgoing, and other kids liked that the way some kids liked Bart Simpson. I felt like I was on top of the world when a pretty girl named Cheryl and I were named king and queen of the school—though if the teachers had voted, I'm pretty sure Cheryl would've been crowned standing beside someone else! Anyway, the next year Cheryl and I were voted in *again* and I decided it was time for the king to give the queen a kiss on the cheek. That's probably the hardest a girl ever hit me in the face. Explaining to my mother what had happened was worse.

I must say I learned a bit of a lesson that day. God doesn't promise to give anyone everything they want — whether they are kids or kings!

At home, with six brothers and sisters, nobody thought of me as a king. We were all just family. When I look at a lot of modern families today — families you never see sitting together outside as the sun goes down, sharing homemade tea and stories with their neighbors — I'm not surprised so many of them have trouble visualizing what it's like to be part of God's Heavenly Family.

I realize now how fortunate I was to spend so much time together with my brothers and sisters as kids. I was so lucky that my mom made sure we shared time with our church friends as much as possible. I wrote earlier about the discipline and the high moral standards of my church and my community, and it was in those afternoons and evenings of talking together that the bonds were forged that could support all of us in times of need.

The bond with Christian friends is a special bond in our walk through life and an invaluable aid as we learn to walk in His presence. The love, loyalty and trust in those priceless friendships prepares our hearts and minds for the love, loyalty and trust we must develop in our Heavenly Father. This is another reason to strive to be a good and true friend—your friendship with others is a small but brilliant reflection of the love God has for them.

How God Proves His Love

Now if we are children, then we are heirs — heirs of God and co-heirs with Christ, if indeed we share in His sufferings in order that we may also share in His glory.
- Romans 8:17 -

The Lord who created all things does not need to justify or prove Himself to us. But He loves us, so He gives us proof of His power and peace when we call to Him with love. That is God's promise. When God calmed the storms after the Flood, it was the dove of peace that landed on Noah's hand, as a sign that God's own peace would be there for those who would reach for Him. That promise still holds true. When we are in Christ, we are God's children as Christ was, and heirs to all God's kingdom.

Of course, I said earlier that even kings don't always get exactly what they want, right? That's because even the best of us cannot see the workings of God's plan. Romans 8:28 tells us, "And we know that for those who love God all things work together for

good, for those who are called according to his purpose." As my mother told me and as later I told my
own child, that means that all things work together for
good, even if we can't immediately see what that
good might be. This is God's promise for those who
walk with Him in their hearts.

It's a hard promise to remember when things are
tough. Even the Bible admits that we frail humans cannot comprehend the majesty of God's divine plan:

*"My thoughts are nothing like your thoughts," says the
Lord, and my ways are far beyond anything you could imag-
ine."*
- Isaiah 55:8 –

God is not a liar. He delivers on his promises, even
if we do not always understand his methods. This is
a little like trying to figure out why people in charge
of things do what they do. Really, the only way to
know why some people act as they do is to live in their
shoes. We can never be God or live in His shoes, so it
is impossible for us to understand his plan.

I remind myself and others more often than I'd
like that everything, absolutely, without doubt, is
working out for our good, just as it says in Romans.
Look back at a problem that seemed unbearable when
you were in school or in crisis. Chances are, there was
a lesson there that helped you avoid a harder problem

later in life. Maybe losing one job leads you to the career of your dreams. A painful break--up might have opened the doors to not making the same mistakes later with the love of your life. God is present in us, working all for our good!

When you watch events in your life from the perspective of life as a whole, not a string of unconnected events, you see this amazing Biblical principle at work. You literally have evidence of God's hand helping you shape the curves of your life's path toward the good. This will give you restored confidence that you are going to be okay, and will powerfully strengthen your walk of faith. As it says in Philippians 4:7, "and the peace of God that passes all understanding shall keep your hearts and minds in Christ Jesus." There is no better scripture to remember when you feel weak and fearful or when you feel mentally stressed for any other reason.

The Author of Peace

Even when you accept that God has an overarching plan for your life that is incomprehensible to you, even when you walk with Him in your heart, there will be times you experience fear at what may lie in store for you in the future. It's natural—sometimes life feels like a horror movie, and you're the person who's about to look around the corner into a creepy dark hallway where anything could be lurking. Again, the Bible can help you.

For my moments of fear, I turn to 2 Timothy 1:7 "God has not given us the spirit of fear, but of power, of love and of a sound mind"! This is another of His irrevocable promises to us, that we have the right to a spirit within us of love, power and a sound mind. He has not given us fear at all, in any sense of the word! He gives us a life of potential—if we fear it, we doubt the promise of our own Creator, and we lose the peace He has granted us.

Confusion is man's choice. As it says in 1 Corinthians 14:33, "God is not the author of confusion, but of peace." Paul wrote those words centuries ago during the three years he spent in a bustling city by the coast, a city full of people and faiths from all over the world. There were so many ideas, so many values contrasting between these peoples that arguments and doubts were already causing distress among those who had chosen to follow Christ. Paul's words of calm were to remind all those people that we do not need to live in fear, because peace is our promise as children of God.

When our minds are tired or we cannot figure things out, we can speak this promise out loud and ask God to give us clarity. Having stood by the side of the Christ himself as our Lord removed confusion from so many, Paul knew that Christ's message of love and strength was simple enough for even a child to understand — a confused mind is in no way what God wants for us.

So how do we embrace God's promise? Romans 12:2 tells us to be transformed by the renewing of our mind. Be focused in the present; forget the past, do not worry about the future. This freshness will be like streams of living water to your physical and mental being. We can do this daily and as often daily as needed. It just takes mental training and spiritual action.

Do not be conformed to this world, but be transformed by the renewal of your mind, that by testing you may discern what is the will of God, what is good and acceptable and perfect.

- Romans 12:2 –

CHAPTER III

BUILDING YOUR MENTAL FORTRESS

*Besides this, we have had earthly fathers who disciplined us
and we respected them. Shall we not much more be subject
to our Heavenly Father and live?*

-Hebrews 12:9 -

H ave you ever known one of those children who just could not sit still, who was always poking and prying and getting into everything, whether it was good for them or not? Well, that was me. I'm embarrassed to say I was not always as appreciative of my mother's sacrifices and strengths as I am now. I was a handful both in school and church. But I was taught—through the Bible and through those in my life who lived the lessons of the Bible—the mental approach to transforming that energy into something productive.

Learning to Grow Up

Back then, our church revivals went on night after night for weeks in big tents under the stars, men removing their hats and wiping sweat off their necks, women getting their shoes dusty as they leapt to their feet to sing and cry "Amen!" as the Spirit took them. It was wild but fun for a kid growing up.

When there was no church, there were still lots of rules that required discipline: shorts were forbidden and there was no "mixed bathing" between boys and girls. Naturally, there was also no cussing, smoking, tobacco chewing or even socializing with those that did those things. It was strict, but we needed those boundaries.

If you have a cup of water in a glass, you can drink it, put out a small fire, help nourish a plant or any number of other things. But without the boundaries the glass provides, you just have a mess of water to clean up. The boundaries and discipline that the moral standards of my Pentecostal church taught me helped me grow from a child with a streak of wildness into a young man with a passionate heart. It was the beginning of establishing that mental approach that would help me again and again throughout my life.

By the time I was in seventh grade, some of my friends thought they wanted to be a preacher, and I thought I did, too. Even after high school I went to

Bible College for two years but then did not pursue full-time ministry...God was with me, but I was no longer sure that He was calling me to His service as a minister.

I took heart from the moral lessons I'd learned from my mother's life, and from the discipline my church had taught me. With those, I grew into manhood with the determination and desire to do well—but no sense of direction.

Instead of service in the church, I chose to serve my country in the US Army. For eight years, the discipline and standards of the military helped me define who I was. Still, it wasn't enough. I still had fears and doubts about what I was meant to be and if I was living up to my potential. My inner peace was gone; I had forgotten how to live with Christ as the most important element of my life.

Leaving the Army, I went into the insurance business and found a career where I could be self--employed. I fell in love, married, woke and slept each day like anyone else...but there was something missing.

For more than twenty years, I fought fear and worry and woke most mornings without the confidence only Christ can give. I relied on my job and my income to define my joy and happiness. And in the meantime, years slipped away, and after eight years my marriage failed. I found myself confused by what seemed like a very wild generation of young people.

My story isn't much different from thousands of others. Maybe even yours. The worries and distractions of the carnal world didn't leap out and steal me away from the presence of God. I let them lead me away, step by step, over years, until I felt so far away I felt I didn't have the strength to come back.

But God will give you the strength if you ask Him. And the lessons He set down for us in the Bible can lead you back to Him.

Life's Wake-Up Calls

Everything that was written in the past was written to teach us, so that through the endurance taught in the Scriptures and the encouragement they provide we might have hope.

- Romans 15:4 -

I'd like to say that the failure of my marriage was the wake-up call I needed, and that I came back to God and never left His presence again. But that's not what happened. When I swallowed my pride in earthly things and focused on perfecting my relationship with Christ, my life did become better. And I *felt* better. But no matter how good life was with God, I somehow let the world distract me again and again.

Do you have those distractions? If you take a moment to examine your last few days, how much of what could have been your time to relax in the presence of Christ was spent worrying about things you can't control, or about other people's business, or about work? When my job ended after twenty-two years, I went back into sales and the shift in thinking depressed me. I realized how much of my mind was occupied by work. How little of it was full of peace.

You make known to me the path of life; in your presence there is fullness of joy; at your right hand are pleasures forevermore.
-Psalm 16:11 -

So I began to call upon God in a very intense way. And ever-forgiving, ever-generous, He led me into a deeper study of learning about His presence. For three years, I read everything about God's peace I could get my hands on, and I began to see how the Bible had answers for my problems.

I came to understand how to have a victorious life of inner peace. What I realized is that by staying in His presence I could have continual fullness of joy. I would not always be happy but through it all I could have joy. The more time I spent studying this subject of the presence of God, the more I knew it had to become a serious way of life for me. More than a simple mental awareness of Him, I needed to find a way to instill Him in every moment.

And so the quest began—how could I possibly be in God's presence at all times when I had so much activity to occupy my mind each day?

If God Brings You to It, He Will Bring You Through It

My transformation required several steps and yours will, too.

At first, I looked at the struggle to change from the "old" me to the "new" as a battle. The old me was entrenched within a fortress of worldly expectations, temporary pleasures and lax spiritual discipline. I found the key to breaking down the walls of that fortress in 2 Corinthians 10:4-5:

For the weapons of our warfare are not of the flesh, but divinely powerful for the destruction of fortresses. We are destroying speculations and every lofty thing raised up against the knowledge of God, and we are bringing every thought captive to the obedience of Christ.

What does that mean, "bringing every thought into captivity to the obedience of Christ"? I worked on the process of controlling each thought and I was very deliberate. If a thought came into my mind I took it captive. It requires great patience and great practice to do this. It's easy to let your mind only react to the world, and to act then on those thoughts that come first. Stopping that process so that you can examine your thoughts is more difficult than you can imagine at first. But it can be done.

When you master that moment of examining your own thoughts, it becomes easier and second nature to you. You'll find that it makes you calmer, more able to adapt to situations and less likely to overreact. Many people would just stop there with their transformation, but this is only the first step. Learning how to organize your mind is important, but learning how to use it is crucial, like sharpening the edge of your mental blade so that you can cut through confusion and doubt. The whetstone for sharpening *my* mental blade has been Philippians 4:8:

Finally, brothers, whatever is true, whatever is noble, whatever is right, whatever is pure, whatever is lovely, whatever is admirable – if anything is excellent or praiseworthy – think about such things.

How does this work? I apply the "Philippians" test to each thought that I capture. If that thought is not true, noble, right, pure or admirable – then I discard it by saying, "In the name of Jesus, leave my mind."

Jesus is there for you, and when you call on Him, He will help you to banish the thoughts that cause you pain and that hold you back from achieving the potential God has given you. I know this not just because I saw the truth of it in my mother's life, but because as I became better and better at this, I was able to avoid many recurring thoughts that had troubled me. Petty disagreements with friends, small hindrances or obstacles in my career, decisions I'd made that hadn't gone the way I expected — these things fell away from my mind like dead limbs from a newly renewed tree.

Is pruning my mind of thoughts that don't meet the Philippians test always easy? Of course not. Not all situations are black-and-white. Life is never easy and it never will be. But it can be beautiful and full of joy. So for the times when shunning "bad" thoughts isn't enough to keep the reality of the world from distressing you, there is a third step to your inner peace.

The name of the LORD is a strong fortress; the godly run to him and are safe.
- Proverbs 18:10 –

Instead of a worldly fortress created by my own mind, I invited God to be the wall that shields and protects me. He is a constant force of love in my life, and to keep Him in my thoughts and heart, I simply say, "Jesus, Jesus, Jesus, Jesus" many times a day. This is the name of all names and is very powerful to help us keep our minds on Him.

When we say His name, it takes precedence in our mind. I find that I can have my thoughts on other things and still be calling the name of Jesus in the recesses of my mind, the way a song stays with you even as you go about your day. When my mind drifts and I begin to feel lost, calling His name immediately brings me back and allows me to feel His presence.

This process has taken a lot of practice, but it was my breakthrough to reach the goal of being in His presence. Saying the name of Jesus breaks strongholds when thoughts just seem to haunt us and we cannot seem to stop them, and sets our mind free.

When you master the constant song of Jesus' name in your mind, it relaxes your body and your soul. You know that you are safe in His love, and you can examine other parts of your life that bring you pain or confusion. This is the final mental step, and perhaps the most difficult of all.

Do not worry about tomorrow, for tomorrow will bring its own worries. Today's trouble is enough for today.
-Matthew 6:34 –

In order to live daily, moment by moment, in His presence, I had to clear away the emotional clutter of my past and dismiss the worry about my future from my mind. If the path of our life is a road, these things are the obstacles that slow us or detour us.

And finding constant inner peace through God's presence is not a "one-shot deal." It's like exercise for your soul. I work at it every day and get into His presence early so that I have a chance for a great day.

Each morning when I wake, I erase the problems or worries of the previous day by returning to my Bible and reading aloud from Psalm 118:24: "This is the day which the LORD has made; let us rejoice and be glad in it!" As I feel the peace and confidence God's word gives me, I declare that this is the only day I have and I must make it a great and important day. Talk about a load off my shoulders!

God has absolutely forgiven our past failures. Why should we carry them around? He wants us to have the strength to deal with today and we need all our energy for this day. We can make plans for our future but why should we worry about something we may not see and "problems" that will probably never happen? Even if we see that future, why should we worry about something that is in God's full control? This is what the "walk of faith" is all about, and to me is the hardest thing we have to learn.

As flawed humans, we want to control the world around us and make sure we have all life's mysteries figured out by ourselves, so it can be hard to set aside that desire for "proof" and simply have faith. For me the simplest way is to go back to what the Bible teaches us about growing and strengthening our faith, which is to pray, speak His name and praise Him. It takes faith to do these things, and the more we do them the more our faith grows.

Chapter IV

The Action of Peace

After Jesus had sent the crowds away, He went up on the mountain by Himself to pray; and when it was evening, He was alone. But the boat was already a long distance from the land, battered by the waves; for the wind was contrary. And in the fourth watch of the night He came to them, walking on the sea. When the disciples saw Him walking on the sea, they were terrified, and said, "It is a ghost!" And they cried out in fear. But immediately Jesus spoke to them, saying, "Take courage, it is I; do not be afraid."

Peter said to Him, "Lord, if it is You, command me to come to You on the water." And He said, "Come!" Peter got out of the boat, walked on the water and came toward

Jesus. But seeing the wind, he became frightened, and be-
gan to sink, he cried out, "Lord, save me!" Immediately
Jesus stretched out His hand and took hold of him, and
said to him, "You of little faith, why did you doubt?"
- Matthew 14: 23-31 -

T he mental strength we gain from the fullness of joy found in God's presence also invigorates our physical strength. But just as we must exercise our minds to gain that strength, it is important for us to take action to remain in His presence daily.

Matthew 14:24-31 is a great illustration of taking action. Peter believed he could walk on the water to Jesus. Can you believe anyone would get out of a boat thinking they could walk anywhere on the water? Wow! But Peter believed and he took action and this is what we must do to live in Christ's presence. We must do the daily mental and physical practice it takes to be spiritually minded, to have fullness inside.

How Do You Take Action With Faith?

To gain the entrance into God's presence (which makes your body feel aglow with His Love), there are several actions you can take. For example, stand in your room, or where you can be alone, and picture Jesus walking on the water, his arms outstretched to you. Imagine the land beneath your feet contains all your fears and worries. Then slowly take a step in the physical world as in your mind you step away from that land, onto the surface of the water. Let your faith lift you toward Christ and you will not sink. Imagine one step after the next on the water's surface, your feet dry and your stride even. The waves will become still before you and the stresses of your life will be left behind on the rocky ground. Walk to Him, and find peace.

Even if physical action is impossible for some reason, you can picture taking the action with your mind and God will grace you with His presence. If I am nervous, I sometimes picture Him sitting at the right hand of the Father as I approach the Throne of God. I know that there I can find wisdom, and in wisdom peace.

But each of us comes from a unique place, and each of us has a different life to lead. What works for one person may not work for the next. So let's go back to the road map. Look through the Bible. Remember the stories that touched you when you first heard or read them. What in those verses caught your attention? You may find the key to God's presence in imagining yourself as part of them: If you are troubled with children as wild as I once was, then try imagining being that type of a child, finding a new kind of quiet wonder on a hot day as you sit in the shade of a palm tree, cross-legged at Jesus' feet with other children as He smiles and welcomes you close. If you feel trapped and alone in a dark place, imagine those three days with our Lord in the darkness of the cave as He waited in gentle patience for the boulder to be rolled free so that He could reveal God's mercy to the world.

We can all create ways to occupy our mind with the things of the Lord, and the tools to do that are in the Bible He gave us.

The Sinking Feeling

As I said before, the world isn't perfect and neither are any of us. And sometimes even the strongest of us break.

When I was seventeen, my mom called me and my brothers and sisters in to say she was no longer able to take care of us. For a woman who had been so beautiful, she was now bone--thin and grey from depression. A light had gone out of her eyes. She had tried to fight the difficulties and the challenges of her life with good grace and perseverance, but they had overwhelmed her at last and she could not find a way to break free from them. It seemed our family was about to be torn apart in ways we had never imagined.

Today, many families face the same terrible situation. Money is the common problem, but anything from a job change to a drug addiction can have an unexpected impact. Too often, families turn on each other just when they need one another the most. We were determined not to let that happen to our mother.

Our pastor counseled her and all of us kids prayed

for her and found ways to help her. We picked up extra chores, looked for ways to add money to the household funds from even the smallest of errands. We shared clothes as we outgrew them and used every scrap of food. And we prayed. We prayed so hard our hands hurt from squeezing them together. We held our mother in our hearts and begged God to let her feel His love strengthening her. And with God's help, we began to see her move forward.

There were few moments in my teenage years as happy as the one when I saw her first unclouded smile. She began to again look and sound like the mom we knew as her courage and strength began to return. Only God could produce this regenerated mom that we were seeing. And how did we know He had brought our mother full--spirited back to us? When she was back to yelling at us about not being late for church!

Where the Spirit of the Lord is, there is liberty.
- 2 Corinthians 3:17 -

Despite the fact that her situation had not changed, my mother's fears disappeared, and those worries were replaced by the peace only the Lord can give. She was then able to "get back in the ring" and go about her life, forever freed from the bondage of overwhelming depression. She gets low at times as most of us do, but never that low again—in Jesus' name she was liberated! And now she knows how to call on the Lord for the answers she needs.

My mother helped me understand that when she slipped from a temporary sadness to that near-devastating depression, it was partially because she took her eyes off the Lord, just as Peter did. She, like Peter, began to sink.

That's why we must keep our eyes (our mind) on Him. But here's the good news: Even though you are human and you will slip sometimes, all you have to do is remember our Christ, fill your mind with His name and His image, and He will reach out to take your hand and keep you from sinking.

We have full, complete access to the God who created the world. All we have to do is say, "Lord I need help right now," call His name and He responds. This is amazing! Our God will save us a thousand times a day if we need Him to; He will never in any way leave us or forsake us.

From the Pit to the Summit

Truly, I say to you, whoever says to this mountain, 'Be taken up and thrown into the sea,' and does not doubt in his heart, but believes that what he says will come to pass, it will be done for him.

- Mark 11:23 -

For all that our Lord gives us strength to endure the challenges of this world and become creatures of joy in His presence, he is not a spiritual life raft only to be called upon when times are hard. The beauty of our relationship with Christ is that He teaches us not just to survive but to grow and flourish and change. When you live in His presence, each day is an adventure filled with possibility. When you act with the surety of your faith in Him, you can move mountains.

There are other books written on the power of our words and I believe in order to have results in our life we must speak positive declarations if we are to have a chance for success. I cannot fully explain why mountains do not always go away in our life when we speak to them in faith as Mark declares, but I do know that those mountains seem a lot smaller and easier to climb when we believe that with Christ's help we can do it. And remember, if mountains were smooth, we could not climb them!

I also know from experience that we have very little chance to succeed if we do not verbalize and believe. In business and my personal life, I've seen dramatic results in the power of vocalizing your intentions to be the best. When you share the constant peace that living in God's presence can bring, the power of that passion is contagious — try it with your friends and coworkers and see how energized and committed you become. Shout it so loud it wakes up the angels!

CHAPTER V

PEACE DESPITE PAIN

*Be merciful to me, Lord, for I am in distress; my eyes grow
weak with sorrow, my soul and body with grief.*

- Psalm 31:9 -

S poiler alert: No matter how much inner peace you
attain, you will still experience pain in your life.
How you manage that pain is up to you, as my mom
has demonstrated with grace again and again in her
difficult life.

Mom had many struggles as she raised her seven
children, but she found strength in God, her church
family and our long-time pastor. The fifth-born child
of our family was a cute little blond daughter named
Dana. She was special to all of us but in her teens, she
became involved in the drug culture of the 1970s. I
don't know if the drugs caused her mental problems

or if she fell into drugs because of problems just beginning to show, but things went slowly downhill for her as she experienced more and more dramatic emotional swings.

When Dana took the medications doctors prescribed for her, she was like the sister I'd known. She was dedicated to the Lord and went to church frequently. She married her tall, dark, and handsome dream husband and they had a beautiful daughter of whom she was so proud. She would call her siblings and challenge us to do good things for others; she'd work with us to get the things she noticed our mother needed. But Dana's life was uneven. When off her medicine, she was depressed and voices spoke to her. One night before mom's birthday at around midnight, Dana tried to take her own life. My mother found her, talked with her and prayed over her until the ambulance came—but Dana went into a coma and died a few days later.

Ephesians 6:11-18 tells us to put on the whole armor of God so we can withstand anything that comes against us, but watching a family member or friend die is terrible and a true trial on the soul. Even when we arm ourselves with truth, righteousness, peace, faith, the Word of God, and constant prayer, there will be moments that rip at your heart—but not destroy it.

When Dana died, it was the most difficult day of my mom's life. We were all in shock as we gathered at the hospital on mom's birthday. We stayed until Dana passed. She was a Godly person even when forgetting to take her meds, she had lived a good life and had accepted Christ as her Savior. There was no question that she was now out of pain, in the arms of God and had found His Ultimate Presence.

The pain of someone's unexpected death is the most common reason people turn their hearts from God—just when they should be turning to Him. It's so hard to counsel someone going through that seemingly bottomless sorrow.

Proverbs 3:5-6 says that if we trust in the Lord with all our heart and do not depend on our understanding, and if we acknowledge Him in all our ways, then He will direct our path. God wants to show us the way we should live as our specific path that He has planned for us. He will not, however, force us. Only by staying in His presence we can follow His lead.

No one in my family wanted Dana to suffer from the nightmares and demons in her head. But we didn't want to lose her, either. What took time to accept was that this was not our path to choose. Our path had to be one of forgiving Dana her mistakes, remembering her life with love, and being there for her daughter. This was where God led us in that time where all seemed lost, and in accepting it we found peace.

Perhaps God put me there in that room that day to give me the strength to help others through their own pain later. I have mentored men with crises in their lives. One lost his wife to cancer when she was only thirty-nine, and he was so down that it sometimes took my repeated calls and encouragement just to get him out of bed. But today, he knows the peace of God, he is very successful in business and happily remarried. Another friend struggled with alcoholism, and I talked with him three or four times a day for two years. He is fully recovered today and helps others who were addicted. This is how God works, by transforming our personal stories of pain into inspirational stories of faith that inspire others to survive.

CHAPTER VI

FINDING YOUR PATH

Trust in the Lord with all your heart, and do not lean on your own understanding. In all your ways acknowledge Him, and He will make your paths straight.
- Proverbs 3: 5-7 -

A rmed with your new mental and action approaches to living in God's presence and enjoying His constant inner peace, you'd think you'd have the world on a string. Not so quick! God doesn't want us to just throw up our hands and say, "That's it! I don't have to try in my own life because God will take care of it!" My hard-working mother would tell you that's not faith, that's just plain laziness.

She taught me to "talk the way you would like to be and you'll be the way you talk." It's the same thing the Bible challenges you to do: Have the discipline and the standards to help your own cause in life.

If you make a plan in tune with your values to drive your own success, and you stay in God's presence, He will be there to ease you over the rough patches and to see you through the inevitable challenges.

You may think it's easy for me to say that, but it's a lesson hard learned on a hard life road. Walking with God through life is without a doubt the most fun we can possibly have on a daily basis, but it isn't always easy. As I look back I see the amazing ways God had His hand on me guiding me even though I was not always aware of His leading.

Seeking Myself

I did a lot of directionless drifting in my life once I left the Army. I'd signed up in 1968, right after getting married, and I made my way to Fort Polk, Louisiana, for basic training. The base was named for the Right Reverend Leonidas Polk, a local Bishop from the mid--1800s, and the nickname for Fort Polk to this day is still "The Home of Heroes." I didn't feel much like a hero, and I knew this was going to be tough soon as I got off the bus at midnight and the sergeants were yelling at us to line up and shut up. We received a nice "burr" haircut, filled our bags with clothes and each of us hauled a hundred-pound bag on foot several miles to our barracks.

Very quickly, I learned a whole new level of discipline. I also picked up some very colorful new language! But after being stationed with my wife in El Paso and surviving on $102 a month Army pay (and lots of peanut butter and jelly), I realized that I couldn't expect God to hand me my next break. I had to work for it. Over ten months I studied every night, doubled my grade average and graduated at the top of my class. God didn't give me the answers to my tests, but He helped me with strength in those long nights of study.

With better scores and increased inner discipline, I quickly moved from position to position and was able to improve my life and my wife's…and by 1971 we had a son on the way.

Reclaiming Myself

If you're a parent, you know the sudden panic that comes with knowing your child is coming into the world. Suddenly I was re-examining my whole life and wondering what lessons I should impart to the small child who would bear my name. And that's when I realized I wanted my name back.

My stepdad and mom had divorced several years prior and I was more in touch with my real father by then, so we decided to change my name back to my birth name (Glenn David Bourland, Jr.) before my son was born, so he would have his rightful heritage. And on October 29, 1971, Glenn David Bourland III was born at William Beaumont Hospital, Fort Bliss, Texas.

They charged us a grand total of $7 for him, quite an investment!

I returned to Dallas in July 1976 after being honorably discharged from the Army and awarded the Army Commendation Medal. I was glad to be out but would never forget all I learned serving in the military. I had grown up a lot, learned how to be disciplined and felt great about our country and our position in the world. I was and am still proud to have served.

Reinventing Myself

Back in Dallas I continued my career, working in different aspects of sales. On one lucky day in North Dallas I sold a machine to an agent who opened the door to a whole new life for me. He told me I should get into the insurance business, and I became self-employed for the first time.

I'd always wanted to own my business and was excited about this career. I worked from 8 a.m. to 9 p.m. each day, cold calling. I had the desire and work ethic and things worked out well—at my job. Unfortunately, my marriage was not so lucky, and in 1976 I was divorced.

I loved my son and saw him frequently for bike-riding and other fun on the weekends. I tried to replace the love I'd lost with my wife by dating—but the girls I met didn't share my values. I dated many girls in two years and found myself lonely and miserable even though I was surrounded by so-called friends.

Seek the Kingdom of God above all else, and live right-eously, and he will give you everything you need.

- Matthew 6:33 -

Feeling so alone made me intensely aware that we live in a world of confusion and the only way we can be strong and know what to do, where to go and what to say is to have an ongoing dialogue with God. When we speak to Him, He speaks to us by opening and closing doors in our life, by guiding us in subtle ways. We are walking through a jungle and God goes before us if we seek Him first. He takes the fear away as He guides us because we are attentive to Him.

I looked back at my mother's life and how she'd battled with the failure of her marriages. I realized that she had found guidance, as always, in the Bible. She made me see that the emptiness I felt inside could either be filled with problems or with the presence of God—I had to make the choice. I chose God.

God Reveals a Path of Love

I told God that I was miserable and I was going back to church and that I wanted Him to help me find a Christian girl to marry. I went to a church singles group in Dallas and met Rosie, and we started dating in May of 1978. By Thanksgiving, I knew I wanted to marry her. God had led me to love. I felt as if I were the personification of what God said he wanted from me in James 2:22: that my faith and my actions were working together, and my faith was made complete by what I did.

But even on the path God had revealed to me with Rosie, my new life was not without obstacles. In December, just after I had proposed, Rosie woke one morning to discover that she was a bit weak and by the next day felt even weaker. This was so unusual for her that she decided to go to the hospital. The diagnosis: Guillian Barre Syndrome. The mylon sheath over her nerves deteriorated and within a few days she was paralyzed and could only move her head, nose and mouth.

I told her I would help her get through this and then she could decide about making me her husband. Over the next few months I worked each day, went to school at night and then saw her at the hospital. After a few months her nerves began to repair, she started in therapy to learn to walk again and we were married October 6, 1979.

The memory of her courage continues to inspire me. Her dad walked her down the aisle, supporting her as she slowly took one step after another to the front. People were saying, "C'mon, Ro, you can do it!" In her weakness, she would stop and cry and then start again. It took forever for her to get to the front, but triumphantly she made it. I have never been so happy or so proud when she looked me in the eyes and agreed to be my wife.

I had to carry her up stairs on the honeymoon since she was not strong enough yet. But now we've worked together in my office for the last 25 years. She has been a source of strength and joy for me. I asked God for the right person and He led me to her. He knew the path of my life before I did. All of those steps — the Army, the sales jobs, the lessons I learned from my first wife and my son-everything was part of God's path to lead me and Rosie to where we are to-day. Besides all that, Rosie is a great Italian cook and grew up in the same denomination as I did. Her close--knit Italian family has been a further source of strength for me.

It's hard to look back when you're in the middle of one of life's big changes. You can't always see the path you're on, but having faith in God and referring back to the moral map of the Bible will steer you toward inner peace and the life you're meant to live.

CHAPTER VII

TAKE THE FIRST STEP

Therefore we do not lose heart. Though outwardly we are wasting away, yet inwardly we are being renewed day by day. For our light and momentary troubles are achieving for us an eternal glory that far outweighs them all.

- 2 Corinthians 4:16-17 -

Y ou've been through the path of my life with me, the lows and the highs, and I throw it open to you again as an example of the miracle of God's promise. Even in those times when I strayed from His presence, I never left His love.

I live now in a constant wonder, my heart full of peace and my mind amazed at the joy our Lord allows me to feel each day. I have my troubles. I may lose my temper in traffic, get depressed at the news of a friend's illness or worry about how I can balance my time with my work and my family.

If you are still unsure that you can immerse yourself in God's presence and feel the calming power of Christ's unending love, the Bible is still there for you as it has been for me, my mother, our nation's founding fathers and the generations of faithful Christians that preceded all of us.

I have discovered that the number-one way to make life fun is living it one minute, one hour and one day at a time; I make sure that my number-one business for the day is living in the presence of God and keeping my mind on Him.

When you get good at this—and with practice, I promise that you will—you will begin to live in a more relaxed state and you will enjoy the moment, the day and what you are doing at any given time. Others will see you as a happy person who is attentive to life and attentive to those around you.

So when your mind wanders away for whatever reason, bring it back to Him as soon as you can. You can speak to God in a frank and simple way and ask His guidance in everything you do each day as you live moment by moment. It is a methodical, purposeful way to live. If our full purpose is to stay in His presence and we are spending our energy doing this, then He will work out the details of our life because our chasing after Him shows Him that we have faith.

Psalm 42:1 says that "as the deer panteth after the

water, so panteth my soul after thee, O God." When you gain the discipline to keep God in your mind at all times, springs of living water will flow through your soul giving you a continual stream of His grace and love. You will be a light that shines to a hurting world and your example will help Christians and sinners alike who need this message.

Once we have begun to live in this state of God's presence the worst thing that could happen to us is to lose it. So how do you continue to develop as an individual, make mistakes, be exposed to loss and pain, explore God's world and yet stay tuned into him so that no matter what happens today or what surprises you encounter, He will help and guide you?

Making God the center of your world is the critical step. No matter what your job may be or what role you hold in the world, you make choices each day that define who you are and how you feel. If God is at the center of those choices, you have the inner peace that comes with knowing you've made decisions based on His divine wisdom. That's why when we learn to live with God as the center of our thoughts, we find true peace that lasts and cannot be found in any other way. God's peace will not let us down as people or the empty pursuit of material possessions do.

My mother is weak these days and is eighty-four years old now, but thanks to a life living in God's presence, her soul still laughs with the brightness of that young woman playing tennis in the hot summer sun. I thank God for every day I have with her, for she continues to teach and inspire me. I hope you, too, find those people who teach and inspire you to stay in God's presence and be filled with His peace.

When you struggle, as we all will, whisper this to yourself, then louder, then with all your heart until you feel His presence:

Where is our strength?

The joy of the Lord is our strength.

How do we find joy?

In His presence is fullness of joy.

How do we enter His presence?

By putting our mind on Him.

There is nothing more important for us than to practice and perfect our ability to get in and stay in His presence. We are completely forgiven, deeply loved, fully pleasing, totally accepted, complete in Christ.

It's the only way to live.

A final word:
Be strong in the Lord and in his mighty power.
-Ephesians 6:10 -

PHOTOGRAPHS

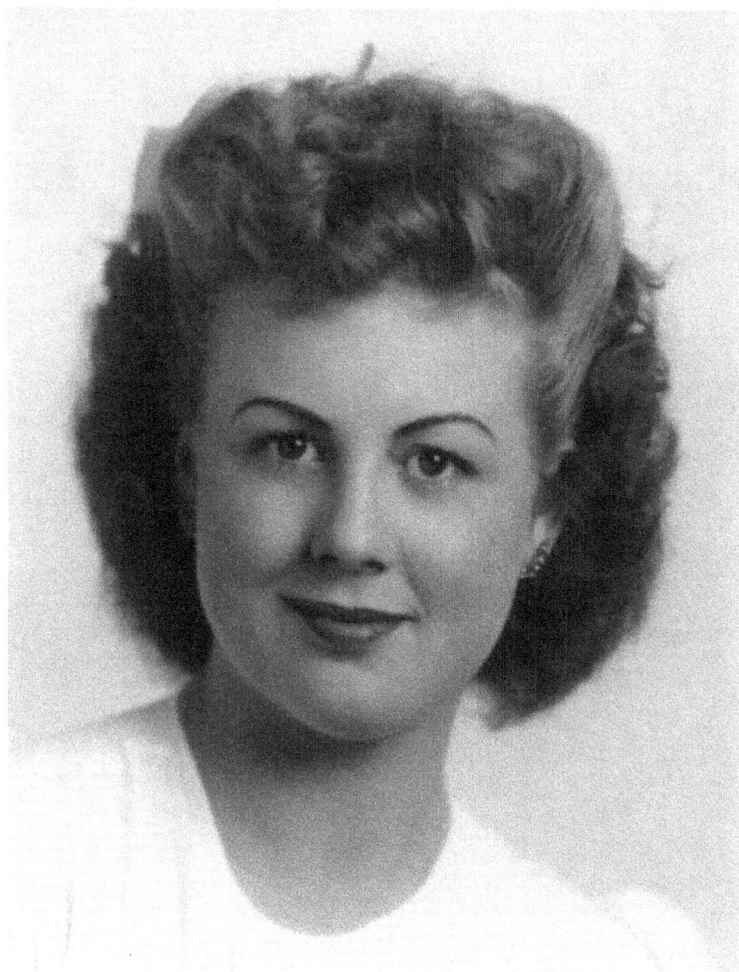

Mom in the 1940s

1995 Picture of Our Family: Jay, Dana, Dave, Joanna
(back), Katie (front), Peggy (mom), Jeanne, Logan

2012 Picture of Our Family: Jay, Jeannee, Dave, Mom,
Logan, Katie and Joanna

2012 Dad, Dave and Mom

Three Generations of Bourlands: Father, Son and Grandson

2014 in front of the Rehab Center where Mom spent a few weeks. Rosie and Darbi pay her a visit.

2014 at Mom's favorite Wal-mart

ACKNOWLEDGEMENTS

T hanks to my Heavenly Father, who is the Rock that never changes: Thank you, Lord.

I say thanks to so many people who have influenced my life and made a difference in my life.

My wife Rosie, my son Glenn, my mom Peggy, and my sisters Joanna and Jeanne, have each been strength and stability for me. Also, my brothers Jay and Logan, and sisters Dana and Katie, who have always been supportive. These are the ones who love me no matter what I say or do that is wrong or right--Thanks Family!!

To all the Dallas, Kansas City and Houston friends and family through the years and also to my friends at Farmers Insurance, thanks for your friendship, love and patience.

To my friend from Bible College who also pastors a local church and helps me in pastoral ways, Rev. Dave Rose, thanks for being there for me!

Many thanks to Dennis McGough, Jeff Hastings and Diane Krause, who encouraged me to get this done — especially to Diane for putting it all together. She assembled a great team, including: Shelly Davis, editor; Christy Fuselli, cover design; and Tiffany Plunkett, writer, who really put my ideas together so that people could understand the message. I recommend these great folks to anyone!

Because of all of you I pray this book will bless and strengthen many!